P9-AER-712
doll
Dining
Serve up
a whole lot
of fun!
er it!
know you want to.
Ice Cream
American Girl®

Published by American Girl Publishing

Questions or comments? Call 1-800-845-0005, visit **americangirl.com**, or write to Customer Service, American Girl, 8400 Fairway Place, Middleton, WI 53562-0497.

Printed in China
15 16 17 18 19 20 21 22 LEO 10 9 8 7 6 5 4 3 2 1

Editorial Development: Trula Magruder
Art Direction & Design: Gretchen Becker, Sigrid Hubertz, Lisa Wilber
Production: Jeannette Bailey, Sarah Boecher, Tami Kepler, Judith Lary, Kristi Tabrizi
Set Photography: Kristen Kurt, Travis Mancl, Jeff Rockwell, Joe Hinrichs
Craft Stylists: Trula Magruder, Lisa Wilber
Set Stylists: Jane Amini, Kim Sphar, Meghan Hurley, Julia Kinney, Marie Sommers
Illustration: Casey Lukatz

Craft with Care

When creating crafts or accessories that will touch your doll, remember that dye colors from ribbons, felt, beads, and other supplies may bleed color onto a doll and leave permanent stains. To help prevent this, use light colors when possible, and check your doll often to make sure colors aren't transferring to her body or vinyl. And never get your doll wet! Water greatly increases the risk of dye rub-off.

Dear Doll Lover,

Going out is always a treat, whether it's to a Sunday brunch with your family, a coffee shop with your friends, or a fancy restaurant for a special occasion. Now it's time to serve up your special style!

You can create a restaurant for your doll—and her friends—using the fun ideas in this book. Look through the kit's supplies to help discover the type of restaurant you want—is it a bistro, a diner, or a bakery? Or it could be a pizza place, a grill, or your very own American Girl Cafe. Create a new place every day.

You choose how to decorate your place and what kind of food to serve. Set up the tables, craft the meals, and hang up the "open" sign. Bon appétit!

Your friends at American Girl

Special Notes:

Younger siblings and pets might not realize the crafted food is fake, so keep it out of their reach at all times.

When you see this symbol, always ask an adult to help you.

Grand Opening

Get your restaurant ready before you open its doors.

Designing the Decor

Before you begin, decide what type of restaurant you want to open. Then decorate to match your theme. What about a Japanese restaurant with black walls and tiny lotus flowers? Or a fifties diner with poodles and musical notes? Or an American Girl Cafe with black-and-white stripes and hot-pink flowers? You could even create one type of restaurant, and then a few weeks later, open a different one!

Picking Your Dishes

Glue pretend food to dishware so that guests can order it again and again. Use the paper plates included in your kit, or use clean lids, food containers, or old doll dishes. For drinking glasses and bowls, use clear plastic caps. Don't glue things to your good doll dishes!

Wonderful Walls

Build your own restaurant furniture. Use pre-scored cardboard display boards for walls. Paint the boards, cover them with pretty paper, or add stripes with colored tape.

Menu
American Girl Place

Set Up

Make your eatery extra special with these supplies and ideas.

Beautiful Booths

1. To make a booth like the one on page 5, glue batting on the top of a tissue box.

2. Cover the box with fabric, taping the edges to the bottom.

3. Glue a foam-core board to the back of the box.

4. For a seat back, wrap and tape fabric around Styrofoam™. Glue to the board.

Tip-Top Tables

For tables, ask an adult to help you trim cardboard boxes so that dolls' legs can slip under them.

Sweet Seats

For low seats, glue batting on craft-box lids, and cover the lids with fabric, taping the edges inside.

Tip:

Put fabric to work as tablecloths or napkins or to make cushions or seat backs. Match colors to your restaurant style. Try a checkered print for a pizzeria or crisp white cotton for an elegant eatery.

Show Your Style

Display the posters or stickers from your kit on the walls to give diners something interesting to look at.

Give Guests a Sign!

Let customers know you're open for business by placing one of the signs from your kit where guests can see it.

Create Candles

Arrange pretend candles on the tables. To make one, tape the candle ends from your kit around a 1-inch Styrofoam™ ball. Cut a drinking straw so that it's slightly lower than the candle's edge, and press it into the ball. Then slip a tissue paper "flame" into the straw.

Make It Special

Surprise your diners with a meal that's not on the menus. Write the special on the chalkboard or wipe-off board from your kit.

Flaunt Flowers

Fill mini jars or vases with tiny silk flowers for the tables. Cut snippets of dried or silk greenery for potted plants.

Tempt with Tents

To sell more desserts, use the table-tent sheets from your kit. Glue or tape three sheet edges together as shown. Display a tent in the center of each table.

Trim Tables

These three tiny tips will help make setting your tables a snap!

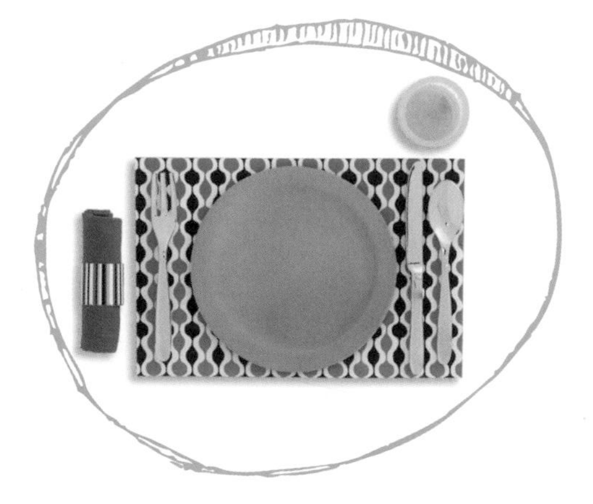

1. Keep linens and tableware straight. Make sure your tablecloth is even on all sides. Line up the place mats with the diners' seats. (Tip: You can flip the place mats from your kit. Use one side for casual dining and one side for fancy meals.)

2. Properly place tableware. "Fork" has four letters, and so does "l-e-f-t," so put forks on the left. "Spoon" and "knife" have five letters, and so does "r-i-g-h-t," so put them on the right. Place glasses above the spoons. Center the dishes on the place mats.

3. Prepare napkins. To make your own, cut 3½-inch fabric squares. Then fold them in half, and place the silverware on top. For a fancy look, attach the stickers from your kit to the napkin corners. You can also roll up napkins and slip the napkin rings from your kit on them or stand them in empty drinking glasses. To make the rings, connect the short ends with adhesive dots.

Wait Tables

To keep guests returning to your restaurant, teach your servers a few basic rules.

- Give servers "Hello!" stickers from your kit so that guests can address servers by their names. Remind servers to be polite and professional throughout the meals and not just when they're handing out the bills!
- When passing out the menus from your kit to customers, let them know if something is not available that day.
- Use the order pad from your kit to write down everything customers request so that they get exactly what they want.
- After guests have "tasted" their food, servers should check on them to see if they're happy with their meals. Make sure your servers pay attention to their customers but don't constantly interrupt their meals.
- Never let a server's hair end up in the food. Keep her hair pulled back at all times.

Italy
Hello, my name is
Alice

Drinks

Serve drinks for breakfast—or any time.

To make pretend drinks for your restaurant, paint non-toxic acrylic paint on the inside of 1¼-inch-wide clear plastic caps. Don't use real doll glasses, because the paint may permanently dry in them! Turn the cap to cover the inside with paint, and then pour out extra paint. Use a cotton swab to clean the cap edge. Allow a few days for the paint to dry completely. You can make soda, milk, orange juice, iced tea, chocolate milk, or lemonade. For a citrus slice, snip to the center of a small craft-foam circle, and glue it to the rim. Shorten a stir straw for a drinking straw. Drop in clear beads for ice cubes.

Just for Fun
Create a few drinks that are half full to show that your guests were thirsty!

Breakfast

Sunny-Side-Up Eggs

Attach a quarter-sized, self-adhesive yellow craft-foam circle to a piece of white craft foam, and cut a wavy circle around it. Attach the egg to a plate with an adhesive dot. Repeat for more eggs.

Wheat Toast

Cut out a 2-inch square from corkboard with scissors. Cut the square into 2 triangles for sliced toast. Attach the toast to a plate with adhesive dots.

Bacon

Cut red craft foam into squiggly bacon shapes, and attach them to a plate with adhesive dots.

Omelet

Cut a 2-inch yellow craft-foam circle for an egg and a 2-inch orange circle for cheese. Cut the cheese in half, and lay it on half of the egg. Add green craft-foam strips for peppers. Dot glue on the inside top edge of the egg, and fold it closed. (Lay a heavy object on the omelet until it dries.) Attach the omelet to a plate with adhesive dots.

Butter and Jam

Cut out ¼-inch squares from yellow craft foam for butter pats. Glue the pats to toast. For jam, squeeze craft glue onto wax paper that's the size of a toast slice. Cover the glue with jam-colored micro beads. Let dry overnight. Remove the jam from the paper, and glue it to the toast.

Croissants

Cut a 2-by-4-inch triangle from tan craft foam. Attach adhesive dots near the pointy end of the triangle, and roll toward the glue to seal closed. (Press the croissants down with a heavy object until they hold.) To shape the croissant, bend the ends in for a few seconds. Glue the croissants to a plate or a gift-tin lid.

Fruit Platter

Pour pink paint into a tiny tin for fruit dip. Add Styrofoam™ for whipped cream. Let dry. Attach the dip to the center of a dish with adhesive dots. For fruit, cut 2-inch craft-foam circles in half, press the fruit stickers from your kit to the foam, and trim around edges. For grapes, run craft glue along a tiny branch, and press on mini purple pom-poms. Let dry. Attach the fruit to a dish with adhesive dots.

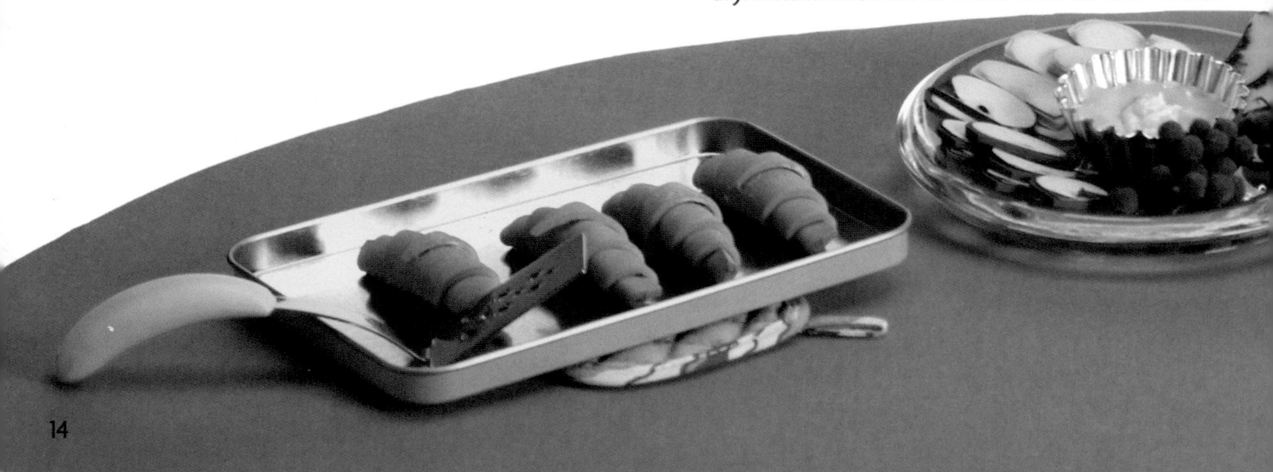

Marshmallow Cereal

Use hole punches and craft foam to make cereal. Punch out brown circles for cereal and colorful shapes for marshmallows. Fill a plastic cap with the cereal, and squeeze on lots of glue to hold the cereal together.

Lunch

Most lunch guests will dart in between noon and 1 p.m.

Pizza

Paint the top of a 2½-inch tan craft-foam circle red, leaving an edge showing. Glue on strips of cream-colored yarn for cheese, small black beads for olives, green craft-foam strips for peppers, and mini red craft-foam circles for pepperoni. Use scissors to cut pizza into slices. Use adhesive dots to attach the slices to a plate, to a stone-colored box lid, or to the pizza box from your kit.

Burgers

Ask an adult to cut a 1½-inch Styrofoam™ ball in half. Paint both ball tops a golden-brown color. Let dry. Press the tops against a hard surface to slightly flatten them. Use a 1½-inch brown craft-foam circle for a meat patty. Cut red foam into a smaller circle for a tomato. For cheese, cut yellow craft foam into a 1½-inch square. Use green crepe paper for lettuce. Use adhesive dots to attach the pieces together, and then attach the burger to a dish or a paper-lined basket.

French Fries

Cut tan craft foam into tiny strips. To make ketchup, pour a dot of glue onto wax paper. Let dry. Cover the glue with red paint. Let dry again. Use mini adhesive dots to attach the fries to each other, and then attach the batch of fries to wax paper.

Mixed Salad

For lettuces, toss pieces of green crepe paper, tissue paper, and crinkle-cut shredded paper in a bowl. Use mini adhesive dots to attach mini red pom-poms to lettuces for cherry tomatoes.

BLT

Ask an adult to cut two 1¼-inch squares from white foam core, and then cut the squares into triangles. With scissors cut a strip of tan craft foam the same thickness and length as the foam core, and glue it to the outside edge of the foam core for the bread crust. Let dry. Use the bacon from page 13. Cut green tissue-paper triangles for lettuce. Cut 1-inch red craft-foam circles in half for tomatoes. Use adhesive dots to attach all the fillings together and to attach the sandwich flat to a plate. Or attach the halves to each other as shown below and then to a plate.

Pickle

Snip off a section of a mini hair scrunchie to make a pickle spear. Attach the spear to a plate with adhesive dots.

Vegetable Sticks and Dip

Use a metallic mini muffin cup or an inexpensive mini tart tin to hold pretend dip. Pour white acrylic paint into the cup. Let dry. Attach the tin to the center of a plate with adhesive dots. Cut orange and lime-green craft-foam strips for carrot and celery sticks. Attach the cucumber stickers from your kit to 2-inch green craft-foam circles. Arrange and attach the vegetables to a plate with adhesive dots.

Potato Chips

Fold cream-colored tissue paper into a number of layers. Cut out a chip shape. Rub the papers to separate them into chips. Leave the chips loose on the plate.

Suppers

At dinnertime, offer a variety of meals—from spaghetti to sushi.

Spaghetti

Fill a pretty candleholder with a single long piece of cream-colored yarn. Squeeze a dollop of red acrylic paint over the center of the yarn to hold it all together. Drop on tiny pieces of green craft foam for bell pepper and black craft foam for olives. Let dry. Press adhesive dots onto the bottom of the dish and then return the spaghetti to it.

Tacos

Cut out 2-inch tan craft-foam circles for tortillas. For fillings, cut strips of brick-colored yarn for meat, green and orange tissue paper for lettuce and cheese, and tiny red craft-foam squares for tomatoes. Fold the tortillas in half, add the fillings, and then glue the inside top edges closed. (Press the tacos down with a heavy object until they dry.) Attach the tacos to a dish with adhesive dots.

Sushi

For each sushi roll, paint one end of a mini spool white. (Look for spools at craft or fabric stores.) Let dry. Roll up a colored paper strip, and slip it into the spool hole. Lay a spool sideways on green tissue paper to mark its width, and cut a 6-inch-long strip. Attach the end of the strip to the spool with an adhesive dot, roll the strip around the spool, and close with another adhesive dot. Attach sushi to a black plastic box with adhesive dots.

Stir-Fry and Rice

Cut craft foam into different shapes for vegetables. Glue tan squares together for tofu. Put the vegetables in a dish and squeeze on lots of glue to hold them all together. For a side of rice, fill a small plastic cap with white beads, and squeeze on lots of glue to hold them all together.

Patio Dining

Serve suppers on a picnic table for an open-air eatery.

T-Bone Steak

Glue two 2-inch brown craft-foam squares together. Let dry completely. Attach the steak sticker from your kit to the foam, and cut around the sticker. Attach the steak to a plate with adhesive dots.

Baked Potato

Wad foil to look like a bumpy oval-shaped baked potato. Attach the foil to a plate with adhesive dots.

Just for Fun

Serve potato fixin's! Use Styrofoam™ for sour cream, craft foam for butter, and green paper for chives.

Corn on the Cob

Remove the paper on a light green crayon and break the crayon into a 1½-inch piece. Color with the broken end to flatten it. Set aside. Knot a 5-inch strip of stretchy cord. Thread on 14 to 16 yellow seed beads, and tie another knot. Run a line of craft glue along the cob and lay the beads on it. Let dry. Repeat with the same number of beads in each row until ¾ of your cob is full. Let dry. Snip the knots, and pull out the cords. Attach the flat side of the corn to a plate with adhesive dots.

Desserts

Showcase desserts for your customers to see!

Sponge Cake

Find a round sponge or cut a sponge into a circle with scissors. For a fruit filling, run a line of red fabric glue around the middle of the cake. Let dry. Attach to a candleholder with adhesive dots.

Pies

Attach adhesive dots inside an inexpensive tartlet pan, and press on tan felt to cover the pan. Trim the edges with scissors. Fill the pan with more felt pieces. Squeeze glue over the felt, and add seed beads. Squeeze on more glue. Let dry. Stretch a Styrofoam™ packing peanut for whipped cream. To make a top crust, weave enough felt strips to cover the pie. Lay the crust on the pie while the glue is still wet. Trim the woven edges enough to tuck them into the pie.

Cookie Tray

Use craft foam for "cookies." To make bar cookies or sandwich cookies, stack and glue 3 rectangles or 3 circles together. For jam cookies, punch out mini hearts from the center of large hearts, and refill the centers with a different color of foam. Or glue smaller hearts to slightly larger hearts. Attach the cookies to a gift-tin lid with adhesive dots.

Petit Fours

Paint mini wood blocks with different colors of pastel acrylic paint. Let dry. Decorate with tiny 3-D stickers. Attach each block to a dish with an adhesive dot.

A G
Bakery

Gear Up

Outfit your chef with an apron and a hat.

Kitchen Apron

1. Fold a 9-by-9-inch piece of oilcloth or fabric in half, with the pattern side up. Lay the edge of the pattern from your kit along the folded edge.

2. Trace lightly around the pattern with a grease pencil for oilcloth or a fabric pencil for fabric. Remove the pattern, and cut around the traced line. Open the apron flat.

3. Cut ½-inch-wide ribbon into two 24-inch strips. Starting 8 inches down the length of a ribbon strip, bend the ribbon over the arm section on the apron, and attach it on both sides with adhesive dots. Repeat for the other arm.

Chef's Hat

1. For a pouf, fold the sheet of tissue paper from your kit in half. Gather the edges of one side, and tape them into a topknot.

2. Slot the 2 hat bands from your kit together at one end to make a single band. Tape them together so that the flaps are on the inside.

3. Turn the tissue paper inside out to hide the topknot. Gather and tape the other edge along the length of the plain side of the band. Slot the ends of the band together, and tape them closed.

Good Service

The job doesn't end until the customer is satisfied.

Box Up Leftovers

Create half portions of food for guests who don't "finish." Attach the portions to the take-out boxes from your kit with adhesive dots. (Pull out the box, and follow the instructions to make it.)

Present the Check

Use the guest-check folder from your kit to present the bill for the meal. Guests will pay the bill using lots of different currencies. They might hand over the cash, coupons, gift cards, frequent-diner cards, or debit cards from your kit.

Sweet Ending

Offer your customers mini mints at the end of their meals.

Dinner Mints

Present mints with your customer's bill. To make a mint, wad up a tiny white paper ball, and wrap it in green cellophane, twisting each end closed.

Order Up!

Serve us your doll dining ideas.

Write to

Doll Dining Editor
American Girl
8400 Fairway Place
Middleton, WI 53562

(All comments and suggestions received by American Girl may be used without compensation or acknowledgment. Sorry, but photos can't be returned.)

Here are some other American Girl books you might like:

Doll School

Doll Art Studio

Doll Tees Felt Fashions

Doll Travel

Doll at Work